The Days That Follow

Readings on the Life and Death of a Loved One

Rabbi Shawn B. Zell

Scribal
Scion
Publishing

The Days That Follow:
Readings on the Life and Death of a Loved One
Rabbi Shawn B. Zell

ISBN-13: 979-8-88665-009-9, Paperback

Published by Scribal Scion Publishing
Teaneck, NJ, USA
First Edition, published in 2024

Scribal Scion Publishing is an imprint of
Scribal Scion Publishing LLC

Please visit our website to learn more about us
and our full catalog of books:
https://scribalscionpublishing.com

Contents

Introduction

The Talmud (Tractate Berachot 16b) relates the following incident concerning the second-century Sage, Rabbi Eliezer: When his beloved housekeeper died, Rabbi Eliezer's students came to his home to console him. When Rabbi Eliezer saw his students approaching, he went up to the second floor so that he could be alone. The students followed Rabbi Eliezer up to the second floor. Rabbi Eliezer then headed toward the gatehouse. His students did the same. Rabbi Eliezer then decided to seek refuge from his students in the parlor, but to no avail.

Realizing that his students weren't getting the message, Rabbi Eliezer said to them with more than a modicum of exasperation in his voice, "It's unfortunate that lukewarm water can't burn you." What Rabbi Eliezer meant was that his students were unable to take a gentle hint. However well-meaning his students were, Rabbi Eliezer was in no mood for company.

Not all of us wish to be alone when dealing with the loss of a loved one. Yet, once the Shiva period has concluded, visits from friends and relatives come to an end and most of us do find ourselves alone. Even for those of us who return to work or resume our busy schedules, there are moments of solitude when we realize that pining for a loved one is not restricted to a specific time. It is during these days that follow that we have the inner need to get in touch with our feelings and to reflect.

The readings in this book were composed by me to help the mourner deal with their grieving, both during the Shiva period mandated by our tradition as well as beyond that period of time.

It is hoped that some who are mourning their loss will be comforted by the pages that follow because they will be able to identify with the readings in this book. Others will find that the readings provide them with food for thought which will help them deal with these feelings.

Most of all, like Rabbi Eliezer in the above quoted Talmudic story, the readings will afford mourners the opportunity to find healing, as they sit in solitude and tend to their broken hearts. It is my prayer that the readings in this book bring much needed solace and meaning, comfort and healing to mourners during the days that follow their loss.

Coping

Among the many areas I felt ill-equipped to handle in my early years of the pulpit rabbinate was dealing with the bereaved. After attending several Shiva houses where the mourner belonged to another synagogue, I was both relieved as well as appalled to learn that I was not the only one who was at a loss for words. It took me years of dealing with death in the congregation to feel that I could help those who were grieving in a meaningful way, not only in confronting death, but also in coping with their loss.

"I know how you must feel" is probably one of the most vacuous statements any member of the clergy can utter when attempting to offer comfort to a member of the community who has recently experienced a loss. "Try to keep busy" is probably a close second when it comes to vacuous statements any member of the clergy can offer in response to one who has come for counselling weeks after the loss has taken place.

Experience ought to have taught rabbis and all other clergy that each person is unique in responding to the loss of a loved one. Within that unique experience of each mourner, there are nevertheless helpful suggestions which you, as a grieving individual, should consider. Such suggestions can be found in the reading that follows.

When you died, part of me died as well. And I can't deal with the void that refuses to go away.
So, I decided to write you a letter. I can better understand my feelings if I put them in writing.
Each time I list any complaint against you, I will also note any commendation you deserve.
Focusing on the good and positive in your life will help me get through my mourning over you.

When you were taken from this world, my world was shattered. I just can't pick up the pieces.
So, I decided to search through old photo albums for pictures where you were the main subject.
Each time I find myself feeling blue, I look at pictures of you to see you at various stages in life.
By looking at these photos for as long as I want, I hope to succeed in bringing a smile to my heart.

When you went the way of all flesh, it was as though an indescribable emptiness entered my soul.
So, I decided to play the music that you loved so much and if I can sing along so much the better.
Each time I wish you were here, the tunes trigger special memories and you are by my side again.
Without fail your favorite tunes strike a chord and that's what I need to help mend a broken heart.

When God beckoned you to embark on your final journey, like many others I was hopelessly lost.
So, I decided to look for direction. I found myself going to your favorite places to eat and snack.
Although I wasn't particularly hungry, I suddenly developed an appetite for your favorite dishes.
Others see me sitting alone, but as I savor your favorite dish, I am once again dining with you.

Who'll Stop the Pain

I once received a call from a desperate parent asking me to speak to her daughter. Her daughter had fallen in love with a young man who was from a totally different background. The mother's desperation blinded her to the fact that the emotions of her daughter would not be receptive to the logic of a Rabbi. Perhaps that is why we find expressions such as "having a heart-to-heart talk" and "having a meeting of the minds." Perhaps we can better understand the ageless Hebrew maxim, "That which emanates from the heart enters the heart." The corollary to this maxim ought to be "and that which emanates from the mind enters the mind" … and never the twain shall meet.

It was the Biblical Jacob, overcome by heartbreak upon learning that his favorite son Joseph had been mauled to death by a savage beast, who refused to be comforted. His pain totally engulfed him.

Being engulfed with pain is expressed by the sentiments in the following reading. Only when and if the pain subsides will the individual be able to continue on in life.

My heart has never hurt like this before. Please believe me when I say that it is broken.
How can it not be broken ever since you took a piece of it with you when you abandoned me?
Maybe I am deluding myself as I desperately search for ways to mend this broken heart of mine.
It is impossible for me to deal with tomorrow as long as the pain of today is too great to bear.

My soul has never suffered like this before. Please believe me when I say that it is shattered.
How can it not be shattered ever since I went to pieces when you departed this world?
Maybe I am deceiving myself as I seek various ways to attempt to make my soul whole again.
It is futile for me to go about building a new life as long as the pain of today is too great to suffer.

My very being has never ached like this before. Please believe me when I say that it is crushed.
How can it not be crushed ever since you brought an end to the two of us being inseparable?
Maybe I am being dishonest with myself to think that I can carry on in life as before.
It is useless for me to look for direction as long as the pain of today is too great to tolerate.

My life has never been crushed like this before. Please believe me when I say that it is damaged.
How can it not be damaged ever since you took with you the most important part of me?
Maybe I am being naïve to believe that new opportunities, adventures, and experiences await me.
It is pointless for me to search for new horizons as long as the pain of today is too great to endure.

I Have Every Right To Be Angry

Modern technology and medical science have created an atmosphere where we are led to believe that we have the upper hand as far as regulating our health and wellbeing. When death takes the life of a loved one, it is as though our sense of being in control has been yanked away from us. We are indignant. And indignation is far preferable to sorrow.

I recall being with the wife of the deceased shortly after death had taken her husband from her. Instead of sadness, there was anger. She was angry at her husband for dismissing her pleas to go see his doctor for a checkup. She was angry at the doctor for failing to detect the aneurism that caused her husband's death. She was angry at herself for not being more persistent and vigilant. And she was angry at God for snatching her loved one away from her.

As much as anger is looked down upon, there is a beneficial aspect of anger. Anger lets us avoid having to deal with emotions that have been sublimated. The reading that follows expresses these thoughts.

Do you realize what you did to me by leaving this world the way you did?

Are you aware that you just shattered my world and that part of me has also died?

How am I supposed to carry on with my life now that you are no longer a part of it?

How will I ever be able to find it within me to forgive you for leaving me so helpless?

Do you know that there was a Sage who taught us that the best doctors should go to Hell?

Is it possible that he went through the same agony that I must deal with being bereft of you?

Why couldn't they have detected what ultimately killed you early on in its development?

How will I ever be able to look at a doctor without thinking about the oath of doing no harm?

How could I have been so blind when I never failed to notice any other slight change in you?

Shouldn't I have learned by now that it was your very nature to try to protect me at all costs?

Why couldn't I make you be honest with me so that I would be prepared for this moment?

How will I ever be able to come to terms with the fact that I must now live life without you?

How does one absolve God from taking you away from those who love and need you so much?

Is it in any way fair to require us to retain our faith in a God who failed to deal in good faith?

Why couldn't the Heavenly Judge remove from this world those who are a threat to society?

How will I ever again be able to bring God into my life after He has left such a void in my life?

What Your Loss Has Caused

There is a legend that is told about a cemetery in the United States where some of the tombstones are most unusual. Rather than list the date of birth and the date of death, some of the tombstones list two dates of death. Quite often these two dates of death are years apart. How is this possible?

It seems that the more recent date of death corresponds to the actual date when the person who lies buried was taken from this world. The previous date of death that appears on only some of the tombstones corresponds to the date when the person, out of melancholy or depression, removed himself from participating in this world.

It took only one generation for melancholy or depression to come into this world. When Cain's offering to God was rejected, God counselled him and in essence told him that depression, if left untreated, can bring about disastrous results. Cain chose to ignore divine counsel and ultimately lost all perspective that, with some effort on his part, things would get better.

This reading deals with one who is also in a state of melancholy or depression. Whereas Cain destroyed his brother, this reading talks about one who is on the path to destroying himself.

When you died, I also died. My vigor no longer lives in me as it did when you were alive.
I couldn't wait to spring out of bed each morning so I could spend the whole day with you.
Now that you are no longer here, I find myself spending a good deal of time each morning in bed.
It helps me avoid facing yet another day, knowing that you will be missing from my life.

When you died, I also died. I no longer have any interest to go out and be with other people.
With you by my side, I had no problem mustering the charm and charisma deep inside of me.
Now that you are no longer here, those traits have been supplanted by apathy and lethargy.
If I can't interact with you, then I have absolutely no desire to interact with anyone else either.

When you died, I also died. I no longer have any desire whatsoever to be seen by other people.
You were the one who put a smile on my face and a twinkle in my eyes. Laughter came easily.
Now that you are no longer here, my face remains expressionless, and my eyes are lifeless.
If you cannot enjoy my smile and see the twinkle in my eyes, then why should anybody else?

When you died, I also died. Any hopes and dreams that I once had have fallen by the wayside.
Because of you I hoped that the good times would never end and I dreamed of wonderful things.
Now that you are no longer here, hope has been replaced by despair and dreams have vanished.
If you were denied life, then I no longer wish to participate in life nor do I care to enjoy life.

Why?

As a rookie rabbi leaving for my first pulpit, my father-in-law, also a rabbi, gave me the following advice: "Don't feel that you have to have all the answers." Decades later, "Sometimes a congregant isn't looking for answers" would be the advice I would give to a rookie rabbi of today.

The interrogative "why?" dates all the way back to Job of the Bible. Especially when confronted with suffering or death "why?" has been asked by countless individuals endless times. It was Rabbi Menachem Mendel Morgensztern (1787-1859) better known as the Kotzker Rebbe who remarked "For the believer there are no questions; for the non-believer there are no answers."

Experience taught me that for those confronted by death, "why?" is seldom a question. Instead, "why?" serves as a reaction that expresses several emotions. In fact, "why?" serves as a catharsis for those attempting to deal with life's most difficult burden, death.

A toddler constantly asks her mother "why?" It has been quite a while since I was a toddler.

Yet I also ask "why?" For me "why?" is not a question. For me "why?" is a cry from my soul.

What makes me think that I could understand or accept any explanation given to me by God?

Many who are in great anguish cry. Because I lack tears, this is how I express my pain. "Why?"

A teenager expresses indignation by asking "why?" "It's not fair" is what the teenager is saying.

It's been quite a while since I was a teenager. But I still believe that the world is built on fairness.

What makes me think that I deserve any more fairness than others who have dealt with death?

We are taught that "life is not fair." Why aren't we also taught that "death is not fair"? "Why?"

Adults express hurt by asking "why?" "You have hurt me!" But explanations do not stop the hurt.

Like so many of my contemporaries, there have been occasions where I too have asked "why?"

What makes me think that I have any right to decide that my hurt is any greater than their hurt?

Hurt serves as a rude awakening that relationships were not as secure as we believed. "Why?"

And now as I attempt to deal with your death, I find myself asking "why?" I cry from my soul.

"It's not fair," I protest. I bemoan the relationship that I thought we once had. "Why?" says it all.

What makes me think that there is an answer to my "why?" that will come my way before I die?

Let no one attempt to provide any answer. "Why?" is a question that I intend to ask God. "Why?"

So Sad

Although I was privileged as an elementary school student to have studied the tragic "Bontshe the Silent" by Yitzchak Peretz in the original Yiddish, I was too young to realize that we had our own version of Bontshe the Silent —albeit nowhere as dramatic—in our own community.

He could be found sitting on a chair outside a store. Whenever a customer needed help carrying a purchase out to the car, the owner would stir our Bontshe the Silent out of his complacency to get up and carry the packages. One day I heard that he had died.

There are any number of communities that can lay claim to their own Bontshe the Silent. There are any number of families into which young Bontshes are born. "Bontshes" deserve better lives and better deaths. The reading that follows is dedicated to their memories.

We mourn because if we don't take this task upon ourselves, then there are no others who will.

We never knew about your past, nor were we able to find out any details, not that we tried.

You lived alone and except for your daily routine at the store, you were content to be left alone.

Ultimately, it took your unfortunate death for us to realize that you had a life and that's so sad.

We mourn because we are part of the community and we feel that it is incumbent on us to mourn.

We never knew to what degree being developmentally challenged radically affected your life.

You carried our packages containing our purchases out to our cars, whenever you were asked to.

Ultimately, it took your untimely death for us to express gratitude toward you and that's so sad.

We mourn because you have now become part of our past that we will recall from time to time.

We never knew whether you had family, friends, or even distant relatives that we should have contacted.

You used names and descriptions straight out of the shtetl whenever you needed to identify us.

Ultimately, it took your sorrowful death for you to make a name for yourself and that's so sad.

We mourn because it was beyond you to perceive the heavenly reward that is most assuredly yours.

We never knew that heavenly compensation for a forlorn existence extends beyond storybooks.

You carried with you the very best that can accompany any soul who is about to meet his Maker.

Ultimately it took your tragic death for us to put your tragic life into perspective and that's so sad.

Filled With Regret

As a child, I attended a Jewish Day School. There were seldom more than 15 students in a grade. What were the odds of Sandy and Jeff, classmates of mine, sharing the same birthday? One year, their birthday parties coincided. Like most 11-year-old boys who didn't think much about girls, I went to Jeff's party. When my mother picked me up from his party, she told me that Sandy had called, asking if I could come to her party. It was obvious that only a handful of students had shown up at her party. Years have passed since that incident, but for the last few decades, I have been filled with regret over my childhood indiscretion.

Regret is a byproduct of humanity. It took but ten generations for God to reconsider – some would say regret – having created humans. It was regret that led God to flood the earth and start all over again with Noah and his family. Our Rabbinic Sages share other regrets that plague God daily, such as creating the evil inclination.

Relationships, particularly siblings and spouses, often spawn regret. What happens when regret surfaces while dealing with the death of a sibling or a spouse? What happens when a sibling or spouse regrets not having been able to accept the personality traits of a brother or sister, husband or wife? Such is the regret in the reading that follows.

I sit here inconsolable looking back at the wasted days, months, years, and decades of your life.
You ignored the many talents, awesome potentials and endless possibilities gifted to you by God.
Instead you were content with mediocrity, and you were satisfied with ordinary accomplishments.
You were never bothered how former classmates less capable than you climbed to high positions.

I sit here brokenhearted because you never dreamed of advancing and improving your lot in life.
Your work was commendable, yet you would turn down suggestions to move up to the next level.
It's not that you didn't believe in your abilities, it's that you were complacent with your position.
Others are enthusiastic and hopeful to build a better career; you were thankful for what you had.

I sit here remorseful because I failed to see that all my cajoling and coaxing caused bewilderment.
Just as I failed to understand how you could be content, so too were you baffled by why I was upset.
You never led me to believe that you were the type to let any grass grow under your feet.
How naïve of me to think that I could change you into the success story I felt you ought to be.

I sit here filled with regret because I am unable to appreciate the fact that you were happy with life.
It was beyond me that success lies in personality traits such as honesty, caring, and thoughtfulness.
You could have lectured me about emphasizing all the wrong characteristics essential to society.
How regrettable that it is only now, after you are no longer here, that I realize how blessed I was.

With You By My Side

It has been said that the worst feeling isn't being alone. The worst feeling is that of being abandoned. For close to half a century, there was a Jewish prison chaplain who helped escort a number of Jewish prisoners to the electric chair. In an interview toward the end of his career, he said that he always made a point of reassuring the Jewish prisoners that they would never be abandoned, because he would be with them until the very end.

The Talmud relates a fascinating story about a Jewish Rip Van Winkle who slept for 70 years. When he woke up, it did not take him long to realize that he was bereft of all those who knew him and held him in high esteem. Feeling totally abandoned, he turned his eyes heavenward and pleaded, "Either friendship or death."

It is not at all unusual for a surviving spouse to feel abandoned. In time, however, the spouse must choose between feelings of abandonment or being surrounded by friends, family, traditions, and faith. The reading that follows expresses such sentiments.

Although I must confront life without you, I must never look upon myself as being abandoned.

I have been blessed with friends to whom I can turn. These friends come in all shapes and sizes.

There are those who will invite me for coffee. Some will stop by to visit. Others will place a call.

And even if these friends are hard to find I have my hobbies, my plants, and my books by my side.

Although I must tackle life without you, I must never look upon myself as being abandoned.

I have been blessed with family to whom I can turn. My family spans a period of many years.

There are those who will invite me for holiday meals and will be sure to send me birthday cards.

And even if these family members are hard to find, I have many memories that I can write about.

Although I must face life without you, I must never look upon myself as being abandoned.

I have been blessed with traditions ready to embrace me. These traditions reach back in time.

There are traditions that are rooted in my religion. There are traditions cultivated by our culture.

And even if these traditions hold little meaning for me, perhaps I can begin my own traditions.

Although I must continue in life without you, I must never look upon myself as being abandoned.

I have been blessed with a faith that will provide me with comfort. This faith began in the Bible.

Faith is there for me to make hard times more manageable and good times more meaningful.

And even if I find it difficult to have faith in God, I must always know that God has faith in me.

The Good Times

In Judaism there is a special blessing known as "Shehecheyanu." The term Shehecheyanu translates as "Who (God) has kept us alive". The blessing itself consists of eleven words, and it is recited on certain special occasions, such as eating a certain kind of fruit for the first time during the year. The Shehecheyanu blessing is also recited on the first night of a festival.

There is a story told how, during the Holocaust, the Jews in the Bergen-Belsen Concentration Camp miraculously fashioned ersatz Chanukah candles. The honor of fulfilling the commandment on the first night of the festival was given to the rabbi of Bluzhov. Ceremoniously, he recited the first two blessings. However, he paused before he continued with the Shehecheyanu blessing. When taken to task by an educated agnostic for daring to recite the Shehecheyanu in a hellhole, the Rabbi of Bluzhov confessed that he too had those very same reservations. However, seeing Jews prepared to fulfill the commandment of kindling Chanukah candles despite the possible consequences, the rabbi continued and recited the blessing. He offered up gratitude for the special place in his heart because of God's chosen people.

Special places in one's heart are not limited to precarious events. They exist in the hearts of everyday people who are blessed to be able to look back upon "first times" in a relationship. Quite often those "first times" are also "best times" as seen in the reading that follows.

I'll always remember the first time we met. You weren't the least bit interested in me.

And then I made an offhanded remark about a current news item and you burst out laughing.

I was intrigued why you laughed because you were the first one ever to react in such a fashion.

It was your explanation that earned you an exclusive place in my heart from which you never left.

I'll always remember the first time you took me to meet your family. I was on my best behavior.

I need not have been. Your animated and amusing way of dominating the visit left me speechless.

I was completely astonished at how undaunted you were to bring me home to meet your family.

It was your breezy manner that earned you a unique place in my heart from which you never left.

I'll always remember the first trip that we took together. I already had an idea of what to expect.

Your excitement at experiencing far off places was only surpassed by your wide-eyed enthusiasm.

I didn't know what was more breathtaking, your taking in new experiences or watching your reaction.

It was your sense of awe that earned you a choice place in my heart from which you never left.

Life is such that for many who mourn a loved one, death replaces "first times" with "last times".

"Last times" evoke despondency and sadness, while "first times" evoke nostalgia and gladness.

The heartbroken dwell upon "last times", while the whole-hearted reflect on "first times".

You have my undying love for the many "first times". They will forever remain "good times".

I Try to Understand

Rabbinical school never adequately prepared me to comprehend and deal with family members who were confronted by the death of a loved one. As such, the first few times I walked into the home where a death had just occurred, I was amazed at how "calm" and "collected" they appeared to be.

My inexperience and naivete prevented me from realizing that they were in a state of shock. It was only later in my career, that I coined the phrase "God's anesthetic." The wise words found in the third chapter of Ecclesiastes, "There is a time to weep and a time to laugh", suddenly made profound sense. So too did the Jewish laws and rituals which teach us that mourning begins at burial. Prior to that, the bereaved need time to absorb the blow that death has dealt them, especially when that death has come unexpectedly.

The reading that follows attempts to express what a spouse is experiencing when confronted by a sudden and unexpected loss. It's as though God's anesthetic is saying, "Take time to process what has just happened. You will have an opportunity to articulate your emotions in due time, because your emotions are not yet ready to be conveyed."

Who could have imagined that I'd be mourning a spouse that I married just a few short years ago?
The darling children we produced will go through life with no memory whatsoever of you.
Friends assure me that I will get through this and that the children need me now more than ever.
I try to understand what they are saying, but the state of shock I am in prevents me from doing so.

Who could have known that a heartbreaking situation that befalls others would now happen to me?
I'm waiting for someone to come wake me from this surreal nightmare that I am living through.
People our age are supposed to be building their lives, yet yours has suddenly been destroyed.
I try to understand that there are no answers, but right now I am too numb to even ask questions.

Who would have thought that I am now the topic of conversation among those I barely know?
They are probably speaking about me using terms such as "tragedy", "pity", and "crying shame".
In time I will get used to language such as "unfair", "terrible blow", and "why is this happening to me?".
I try to understand that there are no answers, but at this moment I cannot muster any questions.

Who would have believed that my friends and family suddenly find themselves at a loss for words?
Out of desperation, they fall back on the well-meaning, but hollow, "is there anything I can do?".
Right now a shoulder to cry on is still premature because tears of heartbreak have yet to come.
I try to understand mourning will take time, but ever since I received that call, time has stopped.

Valuing Life Through Death

In my first congregation, I was one of three rabbis in the community. I was particularly close with one of the rabbis, an elderly scholar educated in a renowned eastern European rabbinical academy.

One winter, that rabbi came down with a severe case of bronchitis and I failed to call him or visit. One day he called me. A congregant of his living in an adjoining state had passed away and the rabbi was not up to making the trip to officiate at the funeral. Would I make the trip and officiate in his stead? I was honored to have been asked and went over to his house to gather information about the deceased. Upon entering, the rabbi remarked, "My congregant had to die for you to come see me!"

That rabbi's words have remained with me, because unknowingly, he uttered a profound truth. It is only through death that we are able to properly value life. In life we are bothered by certain behavioral traits of a loved one. One would think that now that the loved one is no longer, we are relieved that we don't need to tolerate those bothersome traits any more. Yet, it takes death, and our being alone, for us to realize how insignificant those traits really were.

Your need for approval each time you shared with me what happened at your work place was disconcerting.

There were so many times I felt like pointing out to you that only small children crave constant approval.

Now that you are gone, I realize that it would have taken so little for me to give you my approval.

The only thing is that I have since learned that no one other than you really cares what I think.

Your constant turning a deaf ear to most things I said to you used to aggravate me no end.

I was always angry at myself for failing to point out how very rude you were towards me.

Now that you are gone, I am aware that much of what I would share with you was pure prattle.

The only thing is that the house is eerily quiet unless I begin to speak to myself.

Your brooding used to endlessly annoy me. You refused to tell me what was bothering you.

I used to become so angry at you for your petulance and not including me in your life.

Now that you are gone, it is loud and clear to me that brooding was your form of communication.

The only thing is because I was miffed at you, I failed to grasp that your silence spoke volumes.

Your loud sipping of hot soup and hot and cold beverages at every meal used to drive me crazy.

I was embarrassed every time we were invited out to eat or had people over for a meal.

Now that you are gone, I am no longer embarrassed. Your sipping has been replaced by silence.

The only thing is that whenever I sit down to a meal, I find that I seldom have an appetite.

Turning to God

Judaism is opposed to anthropomorphism. Maimonides, in his Thirteen Principles, asserted that God is incorporeal. And yet, neither the Torah nor any other books of the Jewish Bible hesitate to ascribe to God various human features. God takes his people out of Egypt with a strong hand and an outstretched arm. Moses reminds the Children of Israel that God spoke with them face to face through fire. Similarly, the voice of God breaks cedars and kindles flames of fire.

Employing such terminology can draw a person closer to the divine, especially when one either wants to be close to God to share a wonderful and joyous experience, or needs to be close to God to handle a difficult and sorrowful experience.

I was once asked to address a class of freshman law students. There had been several deaths among their classmates either through car accidents, illness, or suicide. Rather than fill the students with the Jewish view on death, I chose to read to them how heaven is described in a certain historical novel. It tells of the protagonist giving hope to those around him facing imminent death by assuring them that upon reaching heaven, each one of the group will be personally greeted and escorted by God. The reading that follows depicts a mourner finding comfort knowing that she can turn to God in her moment of distress.

In moments of anger, You have been known to threaten to hide Your face and distance Yourself.
But how could You remain angry watching me trying to come to terms with an irreplaceable loss?
Let me see Your tears as I turn to You in my overwhelming sorrow that only You can understand.
And let my tears comingle with Yours so that I can find comfort knowing that I do not cry alone.

In moments of irritation, You have been known to threaten to hide Your face and keep to Yourself.
But how could You remain irritated as I grapple with issues for which only You have the answers?
Let me see Your furrowed brow as I turn to You in total distress that only You can fathom.
And let me find consolation knowing that what I am now experiencing is in no way abnormal.

In moments of acrimony, You have been known to threaten to hide Your face and stay detached.
But how could You remain acrimonious watching me struggle to deal with what has befallen me?
Let me see You biting Your lip as I turn to You in utter despondency that only You can surmise.
And let me feel Your warm embrace that reassures me that I will find a way out of my dire plight.

In moments of indignation, You have been known to threaten to hide Your face and be disengaged.
But how could You remain indignant as I try to reconcile the feelings of loneliness that engulf me?
Let me see Your sullen cheeks as I turn to You in unrelenting grief that only You can discern.
And let me feel Your heavenly compassion so that together we can weather life's many storms.

Fear Not Death

Theology aside, there are two significant differences between Judaism and Christianity concerning heaven. Christians believe that entrance into heaven is gained through belief in Jesus. Jews believe that entrance into heaven is gained through the performance of "Mitzvot" or commandments.

In American culture, believing that we end up in heaven after our demise, Christians have never hesitated to say that the deceased has gone to a "better place". In this instance, Jews would do well to emulate the Christians. It is unfortunate that they do not, because many Jews in our culture fail to take heaven seriously.

If Jews incorporated heaven into their beliefs, the only difference between them and Christians would be that upon one's demise, Jews would remark that the deceased has gone to the "best" place. The reading that follows reflects such a sentiment.

Fear not death, for in death we will be free of all aches and pains that are inflicted upon us.
It is in life that we encounter bruises, as well as cuts and scrapes, during our childhood years.
And in our twilight years, we fear falling because breaks no longer mend like they once used to.
But in death, other aches will no longer affect us, such as stabs in the back and slaps in the face.

Fear not death, for in death we will no longer sin nor will we stray from the straight and narrow.
It is in life that we end up looking foolish each time we step out of line and hurt others.
And as we get older, very few of us become wiser and bother to learn from our indiscretions.
But in death, only the most heinous sins won't be forgiven, and we will merit heavenly rewards.

Fear not death, for in death we will no longer be separated from our loved ones whom we lost.
It is in life that we fail to appreciate and cherish the love and friendship of others.
And as we get on in years, we wonder whether we will also be missed by the generation that follows us.
But in death, we will be reunited with those who went before us, and we will also meet our ancestors.

Fear not death, for in death we will no longer struggle with a question that has always plagued us.
It is in life that we always wonder about God and are often bewildered by God's actions.
And as we get up in years, we find that there are far fewer questions we have of God.
But in death, we will surely feel God's loving presence, as He holds each of us very close to Him.

I Believe With Perfect Faith

There is a story in the Talmud about an idol worshipper wishing to embrace Judaism without having to commit to arduous study or the necessary spiritual and religious preparation. After being rapidly shown the door by the great rabbinical sage Shammai who desired to convey that "instant Judaism" simply does not exist, the idol worshipper appeared before the great rabbinical sage Hillel.

Hillel's feelings about "instant Judaism" were no different than those of Shammai. However, to placate the idol worshipper, Hillel provided the following soundbite: "What is unacceptable to you, do not foist upon others." With its myriad of statutes and laws, Judaism is fundamentally a religion of limitation and self-control. Perhaps this is one reason why the majority of the 613 commandments are handed down in the negative, thereby instructing us what we must refrain from doing.

Equally as important, self-control begins with belief in an omnipotent God who also sets boundaries regarding what He is prepared to do. The reading that follows serves to remind us that God will not put an end to the grief process, but belief in God will help you navigate through the winding roads of mourning. God will not put a smile on the face of the bereaved, but will be there to wipe away the tears.

I believe with perfect faith that I will be able to overcome the grief and despair that engulf me.
I am aware that the shining sun is enveloped by dreary clouds that time will sweep away.
I realize that my current state of sorrow will become inexorably worse once I give into despair.
I know in my heart that the tearful loss that is mine will in time be replaced by joyful memories.

I believe with perfect faith that I will remain neither angry nor bitter at what has just befallen me.
I am aware that there is nothing arbitrary or random when God takes our souls back up to heaven.
I realize that I am part of an eternal system that is beyond my comprehension and understanding.
I know that I find comfort in having been taught that God's rod and staff are part of the system.

I believe with perfect faith that God is greatly moved when He sees me pained by my loss.
I am aware that God is sad when I am sad, and that God will attempt to ameliorate my pain.
I realize that my hurt will neither change nor prevent certain things that are headed my way.
I know that God has not abandoned me, but is here with me to wipe away all the tears from my face.

I believe with perfect faith that God wants to spare me from any and all further anguish in life.
I am aware that ever since the days of Adam and Eve, humans were not destined to live forever.
I realize that we are here in this world for a specified time and we will experience loss.
I know that lost loved ones will leave gaping holes in our lives, but God will aways be here with me.

This Can't Be Happening

I had been called upon to officiate at a burial. The funeral had taken place several miles away and the Rabbi was unable to take hours out of his schedule to accompany the family to bury their loved one. My role was purely procedural. As the casket was borne to the grave and set on the lowering device, the widow said, "Get out of the casket!" It was quite clear that she was in a state of denial.

Nor was she the first. Lot's sons-in-law refused to believe Lot when he instructed them to prepare to evacuate as soon as possible, because God was about to destroy the city of Sodom, and death and destruction were imminent. They thought that Lot was joking. They were in a state of denial.

So too was the wife in the reading that follows. She believed that her husband would soon walk into the house. She believed that the doctors would soon call informing her that her husband was still alive. She believed that she was prone to letting her imagination get the better part of her. She believed that this was all one big nightmare. Like others, she was in a state of rejection and denial.

This is all part of a bad dream. It has always been others who incur losses of this magnitude.
The two of us were unstoppable. There were so many plans and projects that were on our list.
I just know that I'll hear the garage door open, and I'll look up and see you walk into the house.
And I will be running into your waiting arms so very relieved that this was all part of a bad dream.

This is my imagination getting the better of me again. Why do I always envision the very worst?
Didn't you assure me that those doctors and all their statistics didn't apply to cases such as yours?
Just as the doctors are unable to predict the future, so too did your doctors get it wrong with you.
I'm waiting for them to call, reassuring me that all that has happened was just my imagination.

This is so typical where I let my worst thoughts take over so that I am enveloped by melancholy.
This is by no means the first time where I have let myself focus on a heart wrenching scenario.
Shouldn't I be concentrating on exciting thoughts of the many good things in life that await us?
I can't help but feel that I'll snap out of this stupor and try to avoid letting such thoughts prevail.

This is nothing more than a nightmare. Yet, this nightmare seems to be lasting longer than others.
Isn't it time for this nightmare to be supplanted by daydreams of so many things for us to do?
Hasn't it been said that it's when the nightmare is at its worst, that's when we always wake up?
I pray that I wake up soon and once I tell you about it, you will help me get it out of my mind.

A meditation while visiting the grave of a mother

Being a mother is a matter of biology where a female is able
to bring offspring into this world.
Being my mother defies biology because you did things for
me that were humanly impossible.
Like staying up for 72 consecutive hours until I regained
consciousness after I was hit by a car.
As I visit your grave, I now know that death is powerless over
feats that are humanly impossible.

Being a mother rests on decisions rendered by courts of law
because there are also adoptive mothers.
Being my mother defies any legalities because you went well
beyond what was expected of you.
Like reading all my textbooks that I studied in school so that
you could help me with my classes.
As I visit your grave, I now know that death cannot destroy
the selfless devotion that defined you.

Being a mother is a societal term used to define a relationship
between a woman and her children.
Being my mother is difficult to define because it exceeds the
boundaries of typical relationships.
Like being the one that my friends came to and confided in
because you were so understanding.
As I visit your grave, I now know that death means that your
advice continues to live on in others.

Being a mother is a matter of fate which determined that,
ultimately, I would be your child.
Being my mother defies fate because when it involved me
you would follow your heart and soul.
Like forgoing long awaited opportunities and plans because
you placed my needs above yours.
As I visit your grave, I know that death will never quell my
adoration and dedication to you.

A meditation while visiting the grave of a father

When I was a child, I was disappointed that you never bought
me the latest model bicycle.
Self-conscious, I thought to myself that I will never be a
father who deprives my children.
Now I am able to see how I was never deprived of your concern
and love for instilling values.
Standing here at your grave, I pray that, like you, I am
successful in transmitting these values.

When I was barely a teenager, I was jealous every time I
heard other people singing your praises.
Indignantly, I listened to people tell me that if I grow up to
be half the man my father is ...
Now I am able to see how remiss I was in failing to zero in on
your wonderful personality traits.
Standing here at your grave, I pray that I merit others looking
up to me the way they did to you.

When I was an adolescent, I saw you as old-fashioned and
out of touch with the here and now.
Embarrassed, I thought to myself that I will always keep up
with the rapidly changing world.
Now I am able to see that I can differentiate between
ephemeral and ageless values.
Standing here at your grave, I pray that, like you, I am able
to discern between timely and timeless.

Now that you have been taken from me, I realize how blessed
I was to have had you for a father.
Proudly, I revel in the heartwarming recollections of you that
family and friends share with me.
Now I am able to see just how blessed and enriched my life is
because you were my father.
Standing here at your grave, I thank God that I am your child
as I end my visit with this prayer.

37

A meditation while visiting the grave of a wife

I should have reminded you of all of your wonderful qualities, but I didn't.
I was too focused on the qualities that you lacked, and I felt that I was shortchanged.
I now realize that I was depriving both of us of greater meaning in our marriage.
I stand here consumed with remorse for not having seen just how rich my life was.

I should have shared with you how you were always able to make friends so easily.
I was too busy basking in my serenity, relieved that I didn't have to deal with people.
I now realize that without you by my side, my serenity has turned into loneliness.
I stand here filled with contrition for my failure to appreciate having you in my life.

I should have told you that being your other half made me work harder to succeed in life.
I was too absorbed in vying for your approbation and praise that rarely came my way.
I now realize that you were amazed, but thought that I only valued praise from others.
I stand here overtaken by shame for constantly seeking and pursuing your approval.

I should have let you know how much I appreciated you, and how special you were.
I was too preoccupied imagining how well-off other men must be with their wives.
I now realize that instead of looking at everyone else, I should have looked at myself.
I stand here filled with regret for not having treasured the blessings God bestowed on me.

A meditation while visiting the grave of a husband

You always seemed to know when to ask me how my day was,
and when to remain silent.
That's how I knew that you were concerned about me and
wanted to make things better.
Yet, when I was enraged over something that had occurred
and I was seething and fuming,
Never did you tell me to settle down or to forget it. Who is
going to watch over me now?

You always seemed to know how to ask me what I would be
preparing each day for dinner.
That's how I knew that you were concerned about my doubts
about my culinary expertise.
Yet, when I was about to apologize for a lackluster and
mediocre meal, you made sure to thank me.
Never did you complain about eating fast food or leftovers.
Who is going to watch over me now?

You always seemed to know how to ask me whether I was
feeling blue or was under the weather.
That's how I knew that you were concerned about tending to
all my hurts, aches, and pains.
Yet, when I said that there was nothing you could do for me,
and I just wanted to be left alone,
Never did you feel that I was shutting you out of my life. Who
is going to watch over me now?

You always seemed to know how to surprise me each year
when my birthday came around.
That's how I knew that you were concerned about my feeling
that I was no longer attractive.
Yet, when I would lament that I was no longer that pretty
young lady you once fell in love with,
Never did you forget how to make my heart skip a beat. Whose
is going to watch over me now?

A meditation while visiting the grave of a sister or brother

We shared more than some of our DNA. We shared a special family history. We shared a past.
We were the only two who could mimic Uncle Dave sipping his soup at the Passover seder.
How we feared having to explain to others at the table if they caught us stifling our laughter.
Now you have joined Uncle Dave and others leaving me with unique and priceless memories.

We shared more than an address and a family phone number. We shared our set of code words.
We were the only two who knew that "colossal" was the name we gave to our goofy neighbor.
How was it that we never seemed to run out of our own private stock of words and phrases?
Now you converse in a celestial dialect, leaving me to chuckle when I recall our codewords.

We shared more than meals together at the kitchen table. We shared experiences second to none.
We were the only two aware of obscure hiding places and secret entrances at department stores.
How we enjoyed those unforgettable escapades of yesteryear, not as siblings but as close friends.
Now you are up in Heaven under God's care, leaving me to appreciate that you were heaven-sent.

We shared more than parents and relatives. We shared our hopes and dreams. We shared secrets.
We were the only two who knew how I touched up the scratch I put on the brand-new family car.
How could we have understood each other's temperament better than anyone else in this world?
Now I realize what a gift you were to me, and that is reason enough to miss you more than ever.

A meditation while visiting the grave of a child who died from natural causes

I was deceived. When you were born, people simply couldn't get over how perfect you were.
I wish I could be standing here cherishing the few precious years of life that you were granted.
Instead, I find myself weeping at your grave for the many years of life that you were denied.
Dear God! Please don't give up on me even though I have ample reason to give up on You.

I was duped. I knew that something wasn't right because you were not energetic like your peers.
I wish I had never listened to others and had been assertive, demanding you be thoroughly tested.
Instead of accepting that early detection couldn't have saved you, I blame myself for your death.
Dear God! Please try to have faith in me even though I have long since lost all my faith in You.

I was cheated. Whenever I attended a life cycle event of the offspring of friends, I cried within.
I wish I had brought other children into this world but in my mind they would be replacing you.
Instead of letting God make amends for the innocent life He took, I chose to remain childless.
Dear God! Please place Your trust in me even though I find it so difficult to place my trust in You.

I was shortchanged. I didn't understand that with your death, I could look ahead to my future.
I wish I had the necessary inner strength and wisdom to build on the adversity which befell me.
Instead of mustering my energies to live the life you were denied, I let part of me die with you.
Dear God! Please show me Your much needed compassion, even though I have denied You mine.

A meditation while visiting the grave of a child who died from unnatural causes

Your life has been snuffed out, and I stand here at your grave having cried a lifetime of tears.
In the natural scheme of things children bury parents. Parents aren't supposed to bury children.
Like every parent, this was my worst nightmare. Now I must find the strength to face reality.
Your life has been snuffed out, but my love for you will continue to glimmer for as long as I live.

Your life has been snuffed out, and I stand here at your grave in a state of shock and disbelief.
We read about tragedies such as these in the newspapers because they happen to other people.
Like every parent, I had plans and hopes and dreams for you, but they were not meant to be.
Your life has been snuffed out, but precious memories of you will always glow in my heart.

Your life has been snuffed out, and I stand here at your grave still unable to find inner peace.
I believe that your soul is under God's protective shelter, yet I am neither consoled nor comforted.
Like every parent, I didn't realize how blessed I was, but now I see myself as unjustly punished.
Your life has been snuffed out, but my yearning for you will continue to burn for as long as I live.

Your life has been snuffed out, and I stand here at your grave still finding it so hard to accept.
Others tell me that time heals all wounds, but the wound that is mine refuses to be healed.
Like every parent, I celebrated your achievements, but I realize that I am not like every parent.
Your life has been snuffed out, yet despite the tragedy my faith in God remains resolute.

Mourner's Kaddish
(Ashkenazic)

Yitgadal v'yitkadash sh'may raba

B'olma di vra chir'utay v'yamlich malchutay
B'chayaychon uv'yomaychon
Uv'chayay d'chol bayt Yisra'ayl
Ba'agala u'vizman kariv v'imru Amen

Y'hay Sh'may raba m'vorach l'olam ul'olmay olmaya

Yitbarach v'yishtabach v'yitpa'air
V'yitromam v'yitnasay v'yithadar
V'yit'aleh v'yit'halal Sh'may d'kudsha, brich Hu

L'ayla min kol birchata v'shirata toosh'b'chata
V'nechemata da'amiran b'olma v'imru Amen

Y'hay sh'lama raba min sh'maya v'chayim aleynu
V'al kol Yisra'ayl v'imru Amen

Oseh shalom bim'romav Hu ya'aseh shalom
Aleynu v'al kol Yisra'ayl v'imru Amen

Mourner's Kaddish
(Sephardic)

Yitgadal v'yitkadash sh'may raba

B'olma di vra chir'utay v'yamlich malchutay
V'yatzmach purkanay, viykarayv m'shichay
B'chayaychon uv'yomaychon
Uv'chayay d'chol bayt Yisra'ayl
Ba'agala u'vizman kariv v'imru Amen

Y'hay Sh'may raba m'vorach l'olam ul'olmay olmaya

Yitbarach v'yishtabach v'yitpa'air
V'yitromam v'yitnasay v'yithadar
V'yit'aleh v'yit'halal Sh'may d'kudsha, brich Hu

L'ayla min kol birchata shirata teesh'b'chata
V'nechamata da'amiran b'olma v'imru Amen

Y'hay sh'lama raba min sh'maya chayim v'sava
Viyshua v'nechama v'shayzava urefua ugeula
Uslicha v'chapara v'revach v'hatzala lanu
Ul'chol amo Yisra'ayl v'imru Amen

Oseh shalom bim'romav Hu b'rachamav ya'aseh
Shalom aleynu v'al kol amo Yisra'ayl v'imru Amen

www.ingramcontent.com/pod-product-compliance
Lightning Source LLC
Chambersburg PA
CBHW071546120626
46550CB00006B/2602

* 9 7 9 8 8 8 6 6 5 0 0 9 9 *